The Little Matisse

Discover art as you read, draw and play

Catherine de Duve

in association with the Matisse Museum of
Le Cateau-Cambrésis.

D0897528

To my parents

KATE'ART
EDITIONS

The Young Life of

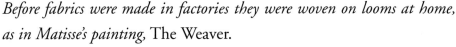

enri Matisse was born in his grandfather's house on New Year's Eve of 1869 in a village in the North of France. His father had a small store and his grandfather was a tanner, who made soft leathers from animal skins. Matisse was born at a time when life in France was changing rapidly. People still travelled by horse and buggy but new railroads were being built, and things previously made by hand were being manufactured in newly built factories.

Before fabrics were made in factories they were woven on looms at home, as in Matisse's painting, The Weaver.

Henri Matisse

Matisse grew up in the village of Bohain, where he went to school, played with his friends and studied the violin. He loved travelling circuses and the country fairs and dances that were held in his village. He wanted to grow up to be a knight or a circus clown, but his father insisted that he go to college and study law. After graduating he worked as a clerk in a law office, a very serious job.

Villagers danced outdoors to live bands on warm summer weekends.

Painting in Paris

When Matisse was 21, he got very sick and needed to spend many weeks in bed. His mother brought him a set of paints to while away the hours. What a revelation! From that time on, his life was never the same. He left his dull office job to go to art school in Paris. *Still Life with Books* was his first painting. The colours are dark and sombre, a common art style at the time. Matisse signed the painting *essitaM .H*, his name spelled backwards.

Create your own unusual artist's signature.

To paint a still life the artist begins by collecting different objects and arranging them in an interesting way.

Plaster bust

Art students in the 1800s learned to draw faces by copying plaster busts like this one. It was less expensive than using live models. Matisse quickly graduated to more interesting work. He went to the Louvre Museum to copy the art of great masters, and he made drawings of Paris street scenes like this one.

Arrange different objects on a table and sketch a still life.

Horse-drawn carriage, 1900

Starving Artists

Matisse and his artist friends lived the life of starving artists. Sometimes they did not have enough money to buy food or a warm winter coat. Matisse lived in a small attic studio overlooking the River Seine in Paris. He climbed 102 stairs to get to his little home. There he painted still lifes of objects he collected here and there, including pieces of broken pottery and odd samples of fabric.

How many different colours can you find on Matisse's palette?

Matisse's art supply table

Sometimes Matisse painted live models in a studio with other artists. Can you find the shadows in this painting and tell where the light is coming from? Each artist sees the model from a different point of view. Matisse paints him from behind and uses shadows to make the curves of his back more dramatic.

How many artists can you find in the painting?

Artists often say that drawing the human body is one of the hardest things to learn. As they make sketches from live models, they learn to observe and depict the form of each muscle. They also learn to capture different reflections of light and patterns made by shadows.

Colour Discovered

In the summer of 1895, Matisse left Paris to paint in Brittany on the Atlantic coast. There he saw the ocean for the first time in his life. He was fascinated by the rolling waves and wild coastline. That summer, he also discovered the Impressionists, who had launched an art revolution by painting simple everyday scenes in the open air. Matisse was inspired by the brilliant colours they used and their lively brush strokes. When he returned to Paris, he no longer stayed indoors to paint. He hopped on his bicycle and went to paint in the country.

spontaneous brushstrokes

H. Matisse—

In 1898, Matisse married Amelie Parayre. For their honeymoon, they travelled to the South of France and to the island of Corsica in the Mediterranean Sea. For the first time, Matisse discovered the bright light and intense colours that he had never seen in the North of France. From that moment on, he filled his paintings with pure and joyous colours. Matisse began to paint from his heart, freeing himself from the rules followed by artists in the past. He was creating his own art revolution.

One day, Matisse saw a blue butterfly. Its colour made him so happy he said it "pierced his heart."

Artists use colours to express emotion. Finish this butterfly with colours that make you happy.

"Crazy Matisse"

Times were hard for Henri and Amelie Matisse. To earn money, Amelie opened a hat shop and Henri took a job painting decorations on the walls of the Grand Palais that was being built for the Paris World's Fair. The construction workers called Matisse "the doctor" because he looked so serious with his neat red beard and round, gold-rimmed glasses. Henri sold hardly any of his paintings. Finally he and Amelie decided to leave Paris with their three young children and return to Bohain, where Matisse had spent his childhood. But the villagers did not understand his art. They would say, "Look, there goes that crazy Matisse."

To get away from their jeers, Matisse moved his family to the town of Lesquielles-Saint-Germain, where they rented a small house on a hill, next to the church. To forget his troubles, he set up his easel between two quiet rivers and painted peaceful landscapes.

Create your own peaceful landscape.

Sunny Colours

Soon the artist's life was again filled with joy and colour. Henri and his family spent the summer of 1904 in Saint Tropez. They stayed with the artist Paul Signac, who taught Matisse the new technique of pointillist painting. To create a scene, the artist makes tiny brushstrokes of different pure colours. Matisse returned to the South of France the following summer. There his paintings exploded with vibrant colour.

strokes of pure colour

H. Matisse

Matisse painted this scene in the middle of a roasting hot summer day. A cobblestone street winds down through the village. The houses vibrate in colours of red, orange, and yellow. In the distance you can see a tall cypress tree and a green hillside. The crest of Mount Canigou is outlined in pink. The whole scene is washed in dazzling, bright sunlight.

Cypress trees *are a common sight in the South of France. They are tall and slender with evergreen leaves that grow to a point at the top.*

Find these details in the painting.

cypress tree   hilltop   roof tiles

cloud   stone wall   cobblestones

Art Shock

In 1905, people in Paris were shocked by a new style of painting used by Matisse and other artists. They painted people's faces in a variety of dramatic colours. They used colour to express what they felt, instead of painting the colours they actually saw. One critic wrote, "The reign of ugliness has arrived... it is an attack on beauty!" Another called the young artists "fauves" meaning "wild animals". The public was not ready for their new kind of art.

Marguerite Matisse at 12 years old

The Fauves *were a group of artists who liked to paint using pure colours right out of the tube. They used different colours as symbols to express the emotion of a scene.*

From the time she was young, Marguerite Matisse was one of her father's favourite models. He did several paintings of her. Here are two of them. How old do you think Marguerite looks in each one? Which one do you prefer?

What facial features look the most similar in each painting?

Marguerite Matisse at about 19 years old

Sculptor

Matisse loved to sculpt as much as he loved painting. In his sculpture of a jaguar devouring a hare, he simplified the forms of each animal. He used a live model for the sculpture of a bearded man that he called *The Serf.* First he made the sculpture in clay. He then cast several copies of the statue in bronze.

 The sculpture in the photo is unfinished. What did Matisse remove in the finished version?

Between 1909 and 1931 Matisse made many sculptures of women in bas-relief. He started by making sculptures that looked more realistic. Over the years, he made ones that were more abstract, with simple geometrical lines.

 A bas-relief is a type of sculpture in which the design projects slightly from a flat background.

Look at the 4 backs and put them in order from 1 to 4, from the most complex to the most simple.

Back no. . . . . . .

Back no. . . . . . .

Back no. . . . . . .

Back no. . . . . . .

Dance

In 1909, a wealthy Russian art collector asked Matisse to paint two large decorative panels for his palace in Moscow. Matisse wanted to paint a scene of paradise on earth. To create *Dance*, he painted with three flat colours: blue for the sky, green for the earth, and orange for the five people dancing in a circle. Moving to the rhythms of a farandole, the dancers express their love of life. But where are the musicians?

 The farandole is a lively and popular French folk dance.

Matisse loved music and dancing. He went to the popular dance halls and cabarets of Paris, including the Moulin Rouge. Perhaps that is where Matisse saw the famous cabaret singer and dancer, Josephine Baker. She dressed in fanciful outfits. One of them had a belt of bananas around her waist.

 Make up a new dance and an outfit to dance in.

Rainy Days

I n 1917, Matisse went to Nice in the South of France for the first time. For a whole month it rained everyday. Alone in his hotel room, with no one else to paint, the artist studied himself in the mirror and painted this self portrait.

 Find these details in Matisse's self-portrait.

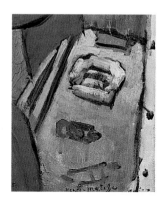

As he painted, Matisse thought of his son and friends who were fighting in the First World War. After a month with no sun, he packed his bags to leave. The next day, a mistral wind chased away the bad weather and Matisse stayed in Nice for the rest of his life.

 The mistral is a powerful, dry north wind that blows in the South of France.

Odalisques

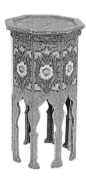

Matisse often travelled to find inspiration for his art. He went to Morocco in North Africa, where he was inspired by the colours, costumes and ways of living he saw there. Matisse loved to walk in gardens filled with strange plants and sip coffee in small cafes. He returned to France with exotic fabrics, objects, and costumes and began to paint a series of imaginary harem scenes, called odalisques.

 A harem is a group of women who live together in a sultan's palace.

What elements in the photograph can you find
in the painting? Is the same woman in both?

Tahiti

Always looking for new things to paint, Matisse embarked on a long voyage in 1930. He sailed to New York to visit his son, Pierre, who worked as an art dealer there. He then continued his journey all the way to Tahiti in the South Pacific.

From the window of his hotel in Tahiti, Matisse took this photograph of a sailboat in Papeete harbour. Later he painted two versions of the scene. Each painting shows a sailboat moored in the harbour. In the distance you can see the island of Moorea, tinged red at sunset.

How many differences can you find in the two paintings?

Cutout Art

Years later, back in his studio in Paris, Matisse remembered the beauty of Tahiti, its clear blue sea filled with fish, corals, sponges, starfish, seaweed, jellyfish and perhaps a mermaid. He had observed the birds so well, he was able to capture them in flight with a snip of his scissors.

Colour Matisse's shapes.

One day, Matisse picked up a pair of scissors and some white paper and cut out a swallow. He put it on a wall of his apartment. Little by little, he covered two walls with images of sky and sea that he remembered from Tahiti.

Did Matisse cut out more jellyfish or more birds? Are any two birds the same?

Jazz

The drum rolls as the ringmaster appears in the imaginary circus created by Matisse. "Ladies and gentlemen, here before you is the amazing sword swallower, about to perform his perilous feat of swallowing not one, not two, but three sharp swords!"

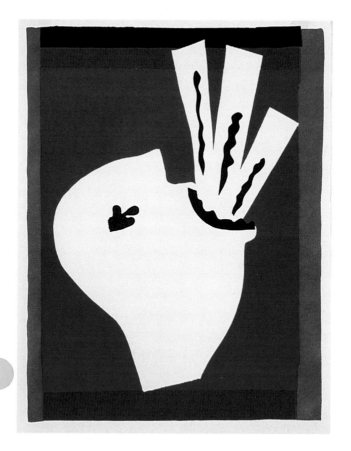

 How many colours did Matisse use in this cutout?

In 1942, a book publisher suggested that Matisse do a book about his cutout art. The book is called *Jazz*. To illustrate it, Matisse made new collages. He drew on his childhood memories of circuses, favourite stories, and trips he had taken.

 A collage *is a work of art made by pasting pieces of paper, cloth, photographs and other objects onto a surface.*

 Make a collage in the style of Matisse. Use coloured paper or white paper that you paint in different bright colours.

Freedom to Paint

Matisse was living in Nice when the Second World War broke out. He feared the city would be bombed so he moved to Vence, a village in the hills. In 1941 he underwent surgery and nearly died. From then on, he painted the things he loved most, including fruit, women, flowers, and this palm tree outside his window. He died in 1954 at the age of 84. By the time he died, he was recognized as one of the greatest artists of the 20th century.

 How many different round shapes can you find?

Draw or paint fruit on this plate.

At the end of his life, Matisse created a masterpiece. He designed a chapel in Vence, creating the stained glass windows, the altar, murals of ceramic tiles on the walls, and even the crucifix. The chapel is one of his last masterpieces, filled with his art and his spirit.

Text: Catherine de Duve
Design: Philippe Plumhans
Published by Kate'Art Editions
Translation: Wenda O' Reilly, Ph. D.

Art Credits:

Georges Pompidou Centre, MNAM, Paris: *The Weaver*, 1895-96: p. 2, *First Orange Still Life*, 1899: p. 8

Matisse Museum, Le Cateau-Cambrésis:

Photographs: Place du Rejet, postcard, private collection: detail, p. 2, Anonymous photograph, c. 1891: p. 4, Matisse working on *The Serf*, c. 1904: p. 16, Matisse drawing an odalisque in Nice, c. 1923-25: p. 23, View of the Port of Papeete taken from the window of hôtel Stuart, 1930: p. 25 *Works of Art: Sword Swallower*, 1947: back cover and p. 28, *Window in Tahiti or Tahiti II*, 1936: inside front cover and p. 25, Jazz, *The toboggan,* 1947: inside back cover, *Self-portrait,* 1951: title page, *Head in profile,* 1891: p. 5, *Horse-drawn cab,* 1900: p. 5, *Studio Interior,* c. 1899: p. 7, *Lesquielles-Saint-Germain,* 1903: p. 10, *Canal bank,* 1903: p. 11, *Collioure, Rue du soleil,* 1905: p. 12 - 13, *Portrait of Marguerite,* 1906-07: p. 14, *Marguerite with Leather Hat,* 1914: p. 15, *Jaguar devouring a Hare,* 1899-1900: p. 16, *The Serf,* 1900-1903: p. 17, *Nude Bak I,* 1909: p. 17, *Nude Bak II,* 1913: p. 17, *Nude Bak III,* 1916: p. 17, *Nude Bak IV,* 1930: p. 17, *Self-portrait,* 1918: p. 20-21, *Maquette of Oceanie, The Sky,* 1946: p. 26-27, *Maquette of Oceanie, The Sea,* 1946: p. 26-27, *Jazz, Monsieur Loyal,* 1947: p. 28

Photo Helene Adant: © MNAM / CCI / Documentation Générale du Centre Pompidou: *Interior of the Vence Chapel:* p. 31

Matisse Museum of Nice: *Still Life with Books,* 1890: p. 4, Art supplies table: p. 6, *Creole Dancer,* 1950: cover, p. 19, *Odalisque with a red box,* 1926: p. 22, *Storm in Nice,* 1919-20: p. 20, Table (Morocco), wood, polychrome, p. 22, *Papeete-Tahiti,* 1935: p. 24, *Still Life with Pomegranates,* 1947: p. 30-31

Photo François Fernandez: p. 20

State Hermitage Museum, St Petersburg: *Dance II,* 1909: p. 18

MANY THANKS TO: Madame & Monsieur Faugeroux, president of the Friends of the Matisse Museum, Dominique Szymusiak, chief curator of the Matisse Museum, Le Cateau-Cambrésis, Wanda de Guébriant et Les Héritiers Matisse, Emmanuelle Macarez, Aurore Delebarre, Blaise Macarez, Sandrine Baivier, Marie-Thérèse Pulvénis de Séligny, chief curator of the Matisse Museum of Nice, Nathalie Lavarenne, Marie Josée Armando, Eric Vaes, Daniel de Duve, Wenda O' Reilly, Joséphine, Johanna, Gabrielle. And all those who have contributed to creation of this book.

Special thanks to the Friends of the Matisse Museum of Le Cateau Cambresis for their support.

www.happymuseum.com